# weblinks

You don't need a computer to use this book. But, for readers who do have access to the Internet, the book provides links to recommended websites which offer additional information and resources on the subject.

You will find weblinks boxes like this on some pages of the book.

## weblinks

For more information about the history of terrorism, go to www.waylinks.co.uk/ series/why/terrorists

## waylinks.co.uk

To help you find the recommended websites easily and quickly, weblinks are provided on our own website, **waylinks.co.uk.** These take you straight to the relevant websites and save you typing in the Internet address yourself.

## Internet safety

↗ Never give out personal details, which include: your name, address, school, telephone number, email address, password and mobile number.

↗ Do not respond to messages which make you feel uncomfortable – tell an adult.

↗ Do not arrange to meet in person someone you have met on the Internet.

↗ Never send your picture or anything else to an online friend without a parent's or teacher's permission.

↗ If you see anything that worries you, tell an adult.

*A note to adults*
Internet use by children should be supervised. We recommend that you install filtering software which blocks unsuitable material.

## Website content

The weblinks for this book are checked and updated regularly. However, because of the nature of the Internet, the content of a website may change at any time, or a website may close down without notice. While the Publishers regret any inconvenience this may cause readers, they cannot be responsible for the content of any website other than their own.

HODDER
*Wayland*

# Why
## are people
# Terrorists?

Alex Woolf

**GALWAY COUNTY LIBRARIES**

*HODDER*
*Wayland*

an imprint of Hodder Children's Books

© 2004 White-Thomson Publishing Ltd

Produced for Hodder Wayland by
White-Thomson Publishing Ltd
2/3 St Andrew's Place
Lewes
BN7 1UP

Other titles in this series:
Why are people racist?
Why are people refugees?
Why are people vegetarian?
Why do families break up?
Why do people abuse human rights?
Why do people bully?
Why do people commit crime?
Why do people drink alcohol?
Why do people fight wars?
Why do people gamble?
Why do people harm animals?
Why do people join gangs?
Why do people live on the streets?
Why do people smoke?
Why do people take drugs?

*J156, 810*
*£15-00*

Editor: Philip de Ste. Croix
Cover design: Hodder Children's Books
Inside design: Malcolm Walker
Consultant: Dr John Gearson, Department of
  Defence Studies, King's College, London
Picture research: Shelley Noronha –
  Glass Onion Pictures
Indexer: Amanda O'Neill

Published in Great Britain in 2004 by Hodder
Wayland, an imprint of Hodder Children's Books

The right of Alex Woolf to be identified as the
author has been asserted by him in accordance
with the Copyright, Designs and Patents Act 1988.

Every effort has been made to trace copyright
holders. However, the publishers apologise for any
unintentional omissions and would be pleased in
such cases to add an acknowledgement in any
future editions.

British Library Cataloguing in Publication Data
Woolf, Alex
  Why are people terrorists?
  1. Terrorism - Juvenile literature 2. Terrorists -
Psychology - Juvenile literature
  I. Title II. De Ste. Croix, Philip
  303.6'25

ISBN 0 7502 4325 2

Printed by C&C Offset, china

Hodder Children's Books
A division of Hodder Headline Limited
338 Euston Road, London NW1 3BH

Picture acknowledgements
The publisher would like to thank the following
for their kind permission to use their pictures:
Camera Press 18; Corbis (cover), 7, 8, 26, 27, 28, 35,
37, 44; Getty Images 41 (Joe Raedle), 43 (Eric
Miller); Hodder Wayland Picture Library 6; Impact
11 (Philippe Achache); Popperfoto 4, 9 (AFP, André
Durand); Popperfoto/Reuters (contents) (both), 5
(Antony Njuguna), 13 (Jamal Saidi), 14 (Dylan
Martinez), 15 (Reinhard Krause), 16 (Win
McNamee), 20 (Dan Chung), 21 (Yannis Behrakis),
23 (Lee Jae-won), 24 (Jose Miguel Gomez), 25, 33
(Sharif Karim), 34 (U.S. DoD), 36 (British MoD), 38
(Sean Adair), 39 (Shannon Stapleton), 40 (Vasily
Fedosenko), 42 (Portland Police Dept.); Rex
Features (imprint page) (Reardon), 10, 12
(Reardon), 29 (Sipa Press, Jon Mitchell), 31 (Sipa
Press), 45; Topham/AP 17, 30; Topham/ImageWorks
22; Topham Picturepoint 19; Topham/Press
Association 32.

Cover picture: 11 September 2001. The World Trade
Center in New York is hit by Al Qaeda terrorists.

# Contents

# 1.What is terrorism?

## What does terrorism mean?

Terrorism is the deliberate use of violence against innocent people to inspire fear for political purposes. It is often the work of small groups who want power. They might want to change the way their country is governed, or to change the world in a political or religious way. It can also be used by governments against people and groups that they view as dangerous.

Most groups who use political violence do not call themselves terrorists. They prefer to describe themselves in different ways – for example as revolutionaries fighting against a brutal government. The government may call them terrorists, but the group might claim that they are the real victims of terrorist acts committed by the people in power.

> 'I consider those actions as a means of spreading our cause. A small group is eliminated, but a great humanity will be created in its place.'
>
> *Abdullah Ocalan, leader of the terrorist group PKK (Kurdish Workers' Party) replying to the accusation that his actions have resulted in the deaths of women and children.*

◀ *In October 2002 Russian special forces stormed a theatre in Moscow to free hostages held by Chechen rebel fighters who had threatened to kill them if their political demands were not met. The Chechens and more than a hundred hostages died in the rescue.*

There is a saying that one person's terrorist is another person's freedom fighter. It is true that there is no general agreement about what terrorism is; it depends on a person's point of view. Many people in the world believe that all acts of political violence, whatever the cause, are unacceptable, and should be called terrorism. However, there are also a large number who support the aims of the people who commit these violent acts. They believe their methods are an acceptable way of changing the way a country is ruled. They would not accept that they are terrorists.

▲ *In November 2002 three suspected Al Qaeda terrorists crashed a car containing explosives into a hotel near Mombasa, Kenya, where Israeli tourists were holidaying. Three Israeli tourists and ten Kenyans were killed.*

**weblinks**

For more information about the meaning of terrorism go to www.waylinks.co.uk/ series/why/terrorists

# The history of terrorism

◀ *The government itself could practise terrorism during the French Revolution, because it had the backing of thousands of Parisians. Here an angry mob hangs a hated politician of the former government from a lamp-post in a Paris square in July 1789.*

The word 'terrorism' was first used in English in 1795 to describe the actions of the French government during the Reign of Terror of 1793-4. This was a very violent stage of the French Revolution, when hundreds of people suspected of being against the revolution were beheaded by guillotine. Terrorism had been used before this time, by governments and small groups, but this was the first time that it was recognized as a political strategy.

During the later nineteenth and early twentieth centuries, terrorism became a favourite weapon of anarchists – people who believed that all government should be abolished. Anarchist groups killed or threatened officials and politicians across Europe and America.

> FACT:
> Between 1894 and 1914, anarchists in Western Europe and America caused the deaths of six heads of state including US President William McKinley who was shot by Leon Czolgosz in September 1901.

During the late 1940s, terrorist groups sprang up in many countries controlled by foreign powers, such as French Algeria and Indo-China. These groups used violence against the troops and officials of the foreign power and tried to force them out. These terrorists were called nationalist terrorists as they wanted their homeland or 'nation' back under their control.

**weblinks**

For more information about the history of terrorism go to www.waylinks.co.uk/series/why/terrorists

Terrorism became more widespread in the late 1960s. Many people had lost faith in their governments, and felt that society was basically unfair. Political extremists formed terrorist groups in countries across Europe, America and Asia hoping to overthrow their governments by bomb attacks, shootings and hijackings. Since the 1980s, the nationalists and political extremists have been joined by religious extremists, particularly certain Muslim groups. They are now the major force behind terrorism in the world.

▼ *A department store in Lebanon is wrecked by a bomb explosion during a 1958 rebellion by left-wing terrorists against the pro-Western government.*

Sometimes governments themselves have used terror to control their people. State terrorism was practised from the 1920s to the 1940s by the Bolsheviks in the Soviet Union and the fascist governments of Germany and Italy. These regimes formed secret police forces, and imprisoned and tortured those suspected of anti-government activities. Modern governments that use state terrorism included the government of Saddam Hussein of Iraq, and the military regime that controls Burma.

# The aim of terrorism

There are three basic aims behind nearly all terrorist attacks. The first is to advertise the terrorist group and their cause. When there is a bomb attack in a public place, or a well-known politician is assassinated, people want to know who has done it, and why. These acts can give a small group huge publicity in the newspapers and on television all around the world, even if only for a short time.

The second aim of terrorist activity is to destroy the peace of a country, and to make its government feel insecure and worried. Terrorists choose their targets carefully to cause the maximum disruption and disorder. They may, for example, choose to put a bomb in a shopping centre, a railway station or a government building. As well as the political damage this can cause, terrorists also hope to cause economic damage. For example they may scare away tourists or businesses thinking of investing money in a country.

▶ An Algerian soldier in the French army guards a group of captured FLN (National Liberation Front) terrorists. During the 1950s the FLN fighters struggled to liberate Algeria from French rule.

8

▲ One of the main aims of terrorist attacks is to cause fear. Here people stand around in shock at the site of a car-bomb explosion in a Jerusalem market in 1998.

The third aim of terrorism is to provoke a government into behaving very harshly. Faced with terrorist attacks, it might strengthen the powers of its police force to arrest and question suspects. It may limit freedom of speech and movement to stop terrorists from recruiting more supporters. By imposing strict controls on the whole country, the government will often make itself unpopular, and the terrorists may get sympathy as a result.

'People refuse to collaborate [deal] with the authorities, and the general sentiment is that the government is unjust, incapable of solving problems and resorts purely and simply to the physical liquidation [destruction] of its opponents.'

*Brazilian terrorist Carlos Marighella describing what can happen when a government overreacts to terrorism*

9

# Terrorism and the media

Terrorism could not work without the media. If terrorists' actions were not reported on television and radio and in the newspapers, they would not have any power to put pressure on governments. This is why terrorism is almost unknown in countries in which the government controls the media. So why does the press go on reporting terrorist attacks?

Firstly, journalists are always on the lookout for a dramatic news story, and few events are more dramatic, or 'newsworthy', than a terrorist hijacking or bombing. Secondly, most people working in the media believe that people have a right to know what is going on in the world. Thirdly, there is a danger that a government might try to stop the media from reporting 'terrorist' acts as a way of silencing its opponents. Journalists naturally object to this form of control. As we have seen, terrorism can mean different things to different people, and it is a useful label to apply to one's enemies.

▶ *The terrorists involved in the attacks on 11 September 2001 certainly got publicity. The event made headlines in newspapers all around the world.*

◀ *The media are naturally drawn to dramatic stories, and for six days in 1980, the siege of London's Iranian embassy by an Iranian terrorist group was played out in the full glare of publicity. A TV audience of millions watched as British troops stormed the embassy and rescued the hostages.*

The free publicity available from the world's media is certainly welcomed by terrorists. However, they have no control over how it is presented. News stories usually concentrate more on their violence than the cause they are trying to publicize. So terrorists use other ways to advertise themselves. Leaflets and newspapers are often printed to explain their aims and ideals. Now the Internet provides terrorists with an easy way of reaching a worldwide audience directly. Some terrorist groups, such as the Lebanese Hezbollah, even run their own radio and TV stations which allow them to communicate directly with their supporters.

❝ 'Whichever way one looks at it, the situation in our country is deeply worrying. The two States [France and Spain] have always used all their instruments – military, political, economic and cultural – to destroy this nation's resources to be free in the future… They consider us their enemies instead of neighbours and prefer to oppress this nation rather than to respect the voice of Basque people in a peaceful way.'

*Excerpt from a 1998 press release from ETA, a terrorist group fighting in Spain for an independent Basque state* ❞

11

# 2. Why do people become terrorists?

## The power of nationalism

One of the causes of terrorism is when a group of people within a country hold very different beliefs from those in power. They are often unhappy with the way they are governed and have stong feelings about their national identity. This group may be unable to further its cause through democratic means, such as by voting for a change of government. Often, there are a few people in these groups who are willing to take violent action.

▼ Terrorist groups often find willing recruits amongst young men and even boys. A young member of the Tamil Tigers is shown here armed with an assault rifle.

Nationalist terrorism can arise amongst a group or people with a common ethnic or cultural identity who wish to form their own nation. In the same way people who were once free, but whose land has been occupied by a conquering power, may be prepared to fight for their independence.

Nationalist terrorist groups include the Liberation Tigers of Tamil Eelam (LTTE). The Tamil are a people without their own country who live in southern India and northern Sri Lanka. The LTTE have carried out bombings and assassinations as part of a campaign to win the Tamil an independent state in Sri Lanka.

*Abdullah Ocalan, the leader of the PKK, at a press conference in 1993. Now in captivity, he is regarded as a terrorist by Turkey, but is a hero to the Kurds.*

The Kurds are another people without their own country. They live mostly in Turkey and Iraq. Iraqi Kurds in particular have suffered because they do not have an independent homeland. They have been attacked with biological and chemical weapons by the Iraqi army of Saddam Hussein. The aim of the Kurdish Workers' Party (PKK) is to establish an independent Kurdistan. They have carried out many assassinations and bomb attacks in Turkey.

**weblinks**

For more information about the different types of terrorism go to www.waylinks.co.uk/series/why/terrorists

## case study · case study · case study · case study · case study

Ahmad is a 27-year-old Palestinian student. He lives with his mother and eight siblings in a small concrete house in Gaza, a territory under Israeli occupation. When he was young, his mother would tell stories of her childhood in their family house in Jaffa (now in Israel), before her family was driven out when Israel was established in 1948. Ahmad is angry that he is treated as a second-class citizen in his own country. He has joined Al-Aqsa Martyrs Brigades, a nationalist terrorist group fighting for a Palestinian state. It was responsible for several suicide attacks in 2002. He says he would rather 'carry out a martyr's mission' than continue to live under occupation.

# Political beliefs

Many terrorists decide to take action because they hate the values or principles of those in power, both in their own country and around the world. These political terrorists can be divided into two major groups: left-wing and right-wing.

Left-wing terrorist groups generally believe that the capitalist economic system, in which industry is controlled by private owners for profit, is the main cause of world poverty. Left-wing terrorists favour another system, known as communism, in which all wealth and property is controlled and handed out by the state.

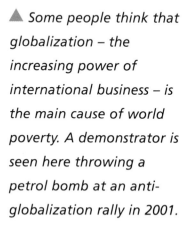

▲ Some people think that globalization – the increasing power of international business – is the main cause of world poverty. A demonstrator is seen here throwing a petrol bomb at an anti-globalization rally in 2001.

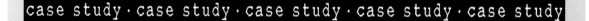

case study · case study · case study · case study · case study

Ulrike Meinhof was born in 1934 in Oldenburg, Germany. As a university student she became involved in the anti-nuclear movement, and went on to become a respected left-wing journalist. Her political views grew more extreme after she interviewed the communist Andreas Baader while he was in prison for arson. She grew to believe that violence was the only way to change society. In May 1970 she helped to free Baader from prison, and together with Baader's girlfriend they formed the terrorist group called the Red Army Faction, also known as the Baader-Meinhof Gang. For the next two years they carried out a wave of brutal terrorist acts across West Germany, including the bombing of office buildings, police stations, and US Army bases. Meinhof was arrested in 1972, and sentenced to eight years imprisonment. She committed suicide in 1976 while still in prison.

Many left-wing terrorist groups were born in the late 1960s in capitalist Europe and America. They included the Red Brigades in Italy, Baader-Meinhof in West Germany, Direct Action in France, and the Weathermen in the USA. These groups were often supported by the communist Soviet Union. They were most active during the 1970s and 1980s, but have been in decline since the collapse of the Soviet Union in 1991.

Right-wing terrorists want to keep traditional ways of life, which they think are threatened by social changes. They often blame social change on immigrants from other ethnic groups. They are usually fiercely patriotic and often racist. Examples include the Ku Klux Klan in the USA, who believe in the supremacy of white people. Right-wing terrorism tends to be on a smaller scale. It is more likely to flare up when people feel their way of life is under threat.

▼ *Extreme right-wing groups, such as the National Democratic Party (NPD) of Germany are a continuing – if small-scale – political force in many European countries. These NPD supporters are taking part in a demonstration in Leipzig, Germany in 1998.*

# Religious reasons

Religious extremists normally believe in traditional moral values. They feel threatened by more relaxed social attitudes to issues such as sex, alcohol, equality of the sexes, and abortion. Religious extremists are especially concerned about the fact that religion is no longer a powerful influence on the way a country is governed. They do not like the way that religion has become a matter of personal choice.

In the USA, most religious extremists are Christian, and are known as fundamentalists. Some have turned to terrorism on a small scale, including the bombing of abortion clinics. In Japan, a religious sect called Aum Shinrikyo has emerged as a reaction against the decline of traditional Japanese culture. Attacks on Israel have led to the rise of Jewish terrorist groups such as Kach, Kahane Chai, who carry out assaults on Palestinians in the occupied territories.

**weblinks**

For more information about terrorist violence in the Middle East go to www.waylinks.co.uk/series/why/terrorists

◀ *Religious extremists like to stress their purity. They urge others to find salvation by repenting their sins and praying. This demonstrator at a religious rally in Washington D.C. claims he is wearing 'the spiritual armour of God'.*

▲ *An anti-American demonstration in Iran in 1979. The placard on the left shows the Islamic fundamentalist Ayatollah Khomeini, who took power in Iran during that year.*

One of the most serious terrorist threats facing the world today is Islamic terrorism. This first emerged after 1979 when an Islamic fundamentalist regime came to power in Iran. This inspired some others in the Muslim world. They were encouraged to try to change their own countries by attacking their 'anti-religious' governments.

The policy of Israel towards the Palestinians is another reason that has led some Muslims down the path of terrorism. Islamic terrorists also launch attacks on the non-Muslim West, especially the USA, for its support of Israel. They view the West as the source of the evil that has ruined their own countries.

" 'The ruling to kill the Americans and their allies – civilians and military – is an individual duty for every Muslim who can do it in any country in which it is possible to do it… in order for their armies to move out of all the lands of Islam, defeated and unable to threaten any Muslim…'

*A fatwah [religious ruling] delivered by Islamic terrorist, Osama bin Laden, in 1998*
"

# 3.What methods do terrorists use?

## Hostage-taking

Terrorism is usually the weapon of the weak. Terrorists have few resources compared to the people they fight against. They must choose their methods carefully to apply maximum pressure to their enemies. One very powerful way of doing this is to take hostages.

Hostage-taking is often used by terrorists wanting a platform to make their cause known to the world. Hostage dramas can drag on for days, or even weeks. This extends the time during which a terrorist is in the spotlight. When terrorists demand money or the release of prisoners, threatening human lives can also be a highly effective way of getting what they want.

◀ *Brian Keenan (centre) was held hostage in Lebanon for over four years between 1986 and 1990 by the terrorist group Hezbollah. He is shown at a rally calling for the release of a fellow hostage, John McCarthy.*

case study · case study · case study · case study · case study

On 16 March 1978, Aldo Moro, president of the conservative Christian Democrat Party of Italy, was kidnapped by the left-wing terrorist group, the Red Brigades, and was held hostage for 55 days. The terrorists demanded that their organization should be recognized as a political party. They also demanded the release of thirteen members of the Red Brigades, then on trial in Turin. The two ruling parties of Italy, the Christian Democrats and the Communists, refused to negotiate. After repeated threats by the Red Brigades, Aldo Moro was murdered on 9 May 1978.

In hostage situations, terrorists often aim to increase the terror and panic of hostages to make them more submissive. One way of doing this is for one terrorist to appear violent and out of control, hitting hostages and shouting at them, while another is calm, softly-spoken and reassuring. This technique was used by anti-Israel terrorists who hijacked an Air France flight in 1976. It was also used by supporters of an independent Croatia, who hijacked a TWA flight a few months later.

▲ The politician Aldo Moro, who was imprisoned and later killed by the Red Brigades in Italy. This photograph was taken while he was being held hostage in 1978.

In order to increase the pressure on a government, hijackers will sometimes kill a hostage. In a hijacking by Islamic terrorists in June 1985, an American passenger was killed. Passengers with Israeli passports were herded into a separate area from the others, and threatened with the same fate. The effect of these actions persuaded the American and Israeli governments to give in to the terrorists' demands.

# Murder and destruction

Terrorists sometimes try to shock governments into action by killing people or destroying property. One favoured method is assassination – the killing of a single, well-known figure, often from the government or armed forces. The aim of assassination is to shock and undermine a government. It also shows that terrorists can strike anywhere, even at the heart of a government.

By choosing assassination, terrorists are showing that they are not blind killers, but can select a target carefully. Rehavam Zeevi, a right-wing Israeli government minister, was assassinated by the Popular Front for the Liberation of Palestine in October 2001, specifically because of his extreme views.

Large bombs, usually planted in vehicles, and powerful enough to destroy a building or devastate a street, are another method terrorists use to cause chaos, panic and fear. Before a bomb attack some terrorist groups, such as the IRA and ETA, give a telephone warning. This is called a bomb scare. They do this to show that their aim is not to kill people but to destroy property.

**weblinks**

For more information about bomb attacks go to www.waylinks.co.uk/series/why/terrorists

▼ *The aftermath of the bomb blast at Omagh in Northern Ireland in which 28 people were killed.*

case study · case study · case study · case study · case study

On Saturday 15 August 1998, fourteen-year-old schoolgirl Una McGurk went into Omagh town centre, Northern Ireland, with a friend for lunch. There had been a bomb scare, and Una's friend left to telephone her parents to tell them she was safe. When the bomb, planted by the Real IRA, went off at 3.10 pm, Una was just a few yards away from it. She heard the explosion, and then everything went black. She was knocked over, but got up again and began walking down the street. She saw dead bodies everywhere. She was drenched in blood, yet didn't feel any pain. Una eventually collapsed, and was rushed to hospital where she remained for eight weeks, recovering from wounds to her feet, arms, legs and torso. The scarring on her face was so bad that two years later she was still wearing a special plastic mask to help the tissue heal. For two years she suffered from depression, and still has recurring nightmares about that day.

Suicide bombers, who first appeared in the early 1980s, are one of the most feared of terrorist weapons because they are willing to give up their own lives, and are hard to stop. Individuals wired with explosives hidden on their persons are very difficult to detect. By positioning themselves in very crowded places, like buses or restaurants, they can cause many deaths. They are most often used by Islamic terrorist groups such as Hamas and Hezbollah against Israeli civilian targets.

▼ *A tag identifying the victim of a suicide bombing in Jerusalem in June 2002. Seventeen people were killed in the attack.*

# Weapons of mass destruction

One alarming threat involves the use of weapons of mass destruction. These are chemical, biological and nuclear weapons which can kill thousands of people at once. Chemical weapons release poisonous substances into the atmosphere that can injure or kill people. Biological weapons release tiny organisms which spread diseases among human, animal and plant life. Nuclear weapons are hugely powerful bombs that kill people and destroy property for miles around the centre of the blast. They also pollute the site with radioactivity that can kill people long after the bomb has exploded.

FACT:
The first recorded use of a weapon of mass destruction by terrorists was the release of sarin, a highly poisonous nerve gas, in the Tokyo underground on 20 March 1995. The attack, which killed eleven and injured over 5,000, was launched by the Japanese religious sect Aum Shinrikyo. They placed containers of the gas on a train during the rush hour, and punctured them with umbrellas before leaving the train.

▶ The scene following the sarin gas attack on the Tokyo subway in 1995. In 1999 a senior member of the cult responsible was sentenced to death for his part in the attack.

Chemical weapons are at their most deadly when used in a confined area, such as a subway system. Both biological and chemical weapons could also be used to contaminate food or drink, or a city's water supply. Biological weapons have even been delivered by post: in October 2001, letters containing spores of a deadly disease called anthrax were sent to the offices of several US senators and top people in the media. Five people died as a result.

Nuclear weapons are difficult to build, because they are complicated to make and have to use certain rare types of material. However, it is possible that after the collapse of the Soviet Union in 1991, some of that country's nuclear material and weapons know-how has found its way into the hands of terrorists.

▲ A South Korean family carries out a monthly civil defence drill. They are rehearsing the evacuation of a building in the event of a chemical attack.

However, the greater danger from terrorists probably comes from the use of nuclear material, not for its explosive power, but for its capacity to poison. Nuclear material is radioactive, meaning it emits harmful rays. If this was released using a conventional or 'dirty' bomb, or even placed in a building's air conditioning or water system, the consequences could be disastrous.

## 4. The supporters of terrorism

# Where do terrorists get their money from?

Terrorists raise money in many different ways. These include the proceeds of crime, such as bank robberies, kidnap ransoms, and drug dealing. They also use legal forms of fundraising, such as charity appeals, business donations and by taxing their supporters. Terrorists are also sometimes given money and other kinds of support by the governments of certain countries.

Islamic terrorist groups benefit from the Muslim custom of making regular charitable gifts, known as *zekath*, at mosques. Many of those who give money do not know that it may end up in the hands of terrorists. The Hamas group raises tens of millions of dollars a year through a network of charity associations operating in the Israeli-occupied territories, Europe and America.

▶ *Two members of the rebel National Liberation Army (ELN) of Colombia. The ELN now obtains most of its funds by helping producers of illegal drugs.*

ETA supporters in Spain hold a flag over the coffin of one of their former leaders. She was killed during a police raid in 1998. As well as drug smuggling, the group also raises money through robbery and extortion.

Charitable gifts are the most important source of finance for Al Qaeda, another Islamic terrorist organization. Some of the charities through which it receives money are just front organizations that hide the real purpose of the fund-raising. Others are genuine, but they have been infiltrated by Al Qaeda members. Al Qaeda also makes money through legal businesses, such as Osama bin Laden's construction company in Sudan.

Nationalist terrorist groups such as ETA (Basque), PKK (Kurds), FARC (Colombia) and LTTE (Tamil) make most of their money through drug smuggling combined with donations from supporters. PKK makes about 86 million dollars a year through these means.

FACT:
The *hawala* underground banking system is a popular way for Islamic terrorists to transfer money to and from bank accounts in secrecy. There are no contracts or printed records that would give evidence of a money transfer, yet hundreds of thousands of dollars can move around the world in a matter of hours. Each person involved in the transfer receives a small commission for playing their part. Provided the different links in the chain trust one another, the money will move from one bank to another as desired.

# States which support terrorism

Sometimes governments believe that it is in their interests to support terrorist groups, particularly when they have a common enemy. A country may not wish to go to war openly with another country, but terrorist organizations can provide a way of attacking an enemy indirectly. This is called state-supported terrorism.

This happened during the period of rivalry between the US and the Soviet Union. This was called the Cold War (1945-1990). Many left-wing groups in Europe, Asia and South America were given money and arms by the Soviet Union and her allies. In a similar way, the Americans provided support and training for right-wing groups fighting left-wing governments in countries such as South Vietnam, Cuba, Nicaragua and Chile.

◀ *Contra rebels patrolling the northern mountains of Nicaragua. This guerrilla force battled the left-wing Sandinista government during the 1980s with support from the USA.*

> " Although it sponsors terrorism, Syria is always careful to seem to be against it. In this broadcast it identifies the Palestinians as freedom-fighters while accusing the Israeli forces sent against them of being the real terrorists: 'Syria condemns terror and will continue to condemn it at every opportunity, but what Israel defines as terror is national struggle against occupation… The Israeli occupation of the territories and collective punishment which Israel imposes on the citizenry is terror.'
>
> *Broadcast by Damascus Radio, 1996*

State-supported terrorism has declined since the end of the Cold War. The US State Department [an official government office] lists several countries that currently sponsor terror. Most of these are Islamic nations. Iran, for example, gives about 3 million dollars a year to the terrorist group Hamas and, it is believed, ten times that amount to Hezbollah. Syria supports the Islamic groups the Abu Nidal Organization and the PFLP, and also provides help for the Kurdish nationalists, the PKK.

Communist North Korea, also on the State Department list, has for many years carried out terrorist operations in foreign countries. In 1983, for example, North Korean agents blew up members of the Burmese government, and in 1988 they destroyed a South Korean airliner.

▲ *A member of Hamas protests at the killing of one of his fellows. Hamas is supported by a network of charity associations in Saudi Arabia and the Gulf States, as well as by Iran.*

# Terrorism and organized crime

Many terrorist organizations have turned to crime, and especially drug smuggling, to raise money. The drugs trade is now the main method by which terrorists around the world get their money. This has led to a growing link between terrorist groups and international crime rings.

There are obvious differences between terrorist and criminal groups. Terrorists are usually driven by political or religious goals. Criminals usually act out of greed. However, they have found ways of working together to benefit each other. For example, the left-wing Revolutionary Armed Forces of Colombia (FARC) and the National Liberation Army (ELN) of Colombia are paid large sums for providing armed security for powerful Colombian drug producers.

▼ *Peruvian army troops search a village in Ayacucho for 'Shining Path' terrorists. Seven provinces in this area were placed under military control in 1982 in an effort to destroy this rebel force.*

Colombian anti-drug police in the poppy fields of the Huila region carrying out a raid on opium producers. Opium poppies are used to make drugs such as heroin.

This sort of work is far more profitable than other forms of fundraising, such as kidnapping and bank robberies – and far less risky. Terrorist groups can also make use of drug smuggling routes to move people and arms secretly into Western cities.

There are other advantages for both sides. Organized crime gangs are often able to bribe corrupt political leaders. Terrorist groups who wish to influence or threaten a government can make use of these people. Similarly, powerful terrorist groups can cause political unrest in countries and so weaken their governments, as they have done in places like Colombia and Afghanistan. This makes it easier for organized crime groups to operate without police or government interference.

> 'The West is exporting to us its corrosive [destructive] culture. We are exporting something back that corrodes their society.'
>
> *Islamic terrorist Osama bin Laden explaining Al Qaeda's involvement in the taxing, protection and encouragement of the opium industry in Afghanistan*

29

# 5. What can be done about terrorism?

## Taking action against terrorism

Countries faced with terrorist attack often try to fight back. This is a tempting thing to do, because it can make a government look strong. It can add to its popularity at home, and deter future terrorist attacks. However, direct military action against terrorist groups is difficult because the terrorists usually work under cover. They also work in self-contained cells far apart from each other. Even if one cell is destroyed, the organization can continue to function. Because terrorists are usually so well hidden, countries often find it easier to put pressure on the sponsors of terrorism rather than attacking the terrorists themselves.

▼ The funeral of victims of the 1986 US bombing of Tripoli, Libya. The US raid was in retaliation for a Libyan-backed terrorist attack on US soldiers in West Berlin, Germany.

> 'We must fight terror wherever and whenever it appears. We must make all states play by the same rules. We must declare terrorism a crime against humanity, and we must consider the terrorists enemies of mankind...'
>
> *Benjamin Netanyahu, former Prime Minister of Israel, from the foreword to his book* Fighting Terrorism *(2001)*

A better way of fighting terrorists is by blocking off their sources of weapons and arms. Countries such as the USA have anti-terrorism laws which make it a crime to give money or materials to terrorist organizations. The authorities can expel suspected terrorists from the country, and ban the manufacture or possession of weapons of mass destruction.

Tough action taken against suspected terrorists can end up affecting the rights and freedoms of everyone in the country. The methods used can include surveillance, imprisonment without trial, even torture. When striking at terrorists in other countries, governments run the risk of killing innocent civilians. These tactics can play into the terrorists' hands by making the government unpopular. However, non-democratic governments, such as Iran, which do not depend on the votes of the general public to remain in power, have used these tactics against terrorists with great success.

*▲ Captured terrorists from the Al Qaeda terrorist group held at Camp Delta in Guantanamo Bay, Cuba in 2002. The use of chains, goggles and face masks led to international concern that the US was mistreating these prisoners.*

# Talking to terrorists

Governments often decide that the only answer to terrorism is to sit down and talk with the terrorists to try to end the violence. However, negotiation has its drawbacks. France, for example, has made deals with terrorists, offering money and political concessions in order to protect Paris from bomb attacks and to get hostages released. This might save lives and property in the short term, but it risks encouraging terrorists to keep doing the same thing. In 1993, France released Iranian terrorists from prison, hoping this would persuade Iran to stop killing its enemies living in France. However, the killings actually increased after this.

◀ Belfast residents get their first look at the 'Good Friday' peace agreement signed in April 1998 by the British and Irish governments, the Unionists and Sinn Fein. This aimed to put an end to IRA terrorist attacks in Northern Ireland by agreeing a peace deal.

Many countries do not like to admit that they talk to terrorists. The official policy of both Britain and the USA is that they do not negotiate with terrorists. Yet during the 1980s, both countries did exactly that. Britain negotiated in secret with the IRA, leading to peace talks in 1994. The USA offered weapons to Iran in the 1980s in exchange for the release of American hostages in Lebanon.

Many governments use a mixture of both force and negotiation. They instruct their army and intelligence services to undermine the terrorist threat, but they also negotiate when necessary. Israel attacks terrorist bases in its occupied territories, but it has also made deals with terrorists on a number of occasions. For instance, several hundred Muslim prisoners were released from its jails in exchange for hostages following a hijacking in 1985.

> 'Each day without a life being taken is a bonus. I now have a two-and-a-half-year-old daughter and another baby on the way. For their sake I want peace. No principle is worth spilling another drop of Ulster blood for. Life is precious; the nightmare has gone on long enough.'
>
> *A Protestant mother from Northern Ireland after the 1994 announcement of an IRA ceasefire – quoted in Laurel Holliday,* Children of 'the Troubles': Our Lives in the Crossfire of Northern Ireland, *1997*

▶ *Thirteen Lebanese men, held prisoner in Israel for more than ten years, are freed in April 2000. They were released in exchange for information about Israeli soldiers missing in action in Lebanon.*

# Protecting ourselves from terrorism

What can we do to defend ourselves from terrorist attack? Governments spend millions of dollars each year on security and intelligence. They use secret agents to get inside terrorist networks. They take action against terrorist assets and funding. They protect their leaders from attack, and guard their borders.

Getting reliable information about the identity, plans and weakness of terrorists is difficult, but it is vital to any counter-terrorism strategy. Intelligence gathering involves the use of high technology, such as satellite photography and electronic bugging equipment. It also uses the intelligence of the people on the ground, taking advantage of their language skills and local knowledge in politically unstable regions.

◀ *A satellite image showing an Al Qaeda training camp in Afghanistan. It was one of the targets of a US missile attack against the terrorist group in August 1998.*

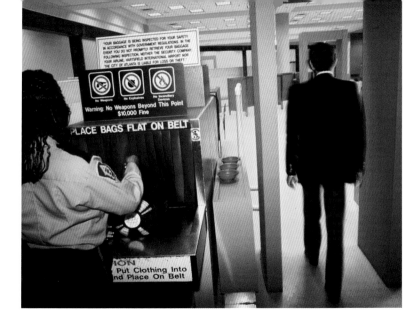

*Aeroplanes are popular targets for terrorist attack. All international airports search passengers and their luggage for concealed weapons before they are allowed to board a flight.*

Co-operation between countries is also vital to counter the threat of terrorism around the world. Governments often work together, signing extradition treaties and sharing intelligence. Nations can also act together by putting pressure on a country that supports terror. For example, they can impose sanctions by refusing to trade with it, or by blocking the export of valuable products like oil.

On a personal level we can also take action to protect ourselves from terrorism in the home, in the street, or while travelling abroad. We can make sure our homes are safe from intruders and properly alarmed, and that we know what to do if we see anything suspicious. We can learn how to recognize a suspect package, perhaps a letter bomb, and what to do if we spot one.

FACT:
During the 1990s spending on counter-terrorism rose dramatically in most Western countries. The US annual anti-terrorism budget rose by more than 50 per cent between 1996 and 2001, to ten billion dollars. That figure rose even higher in 2002 when the Federal Bureau of Intelligence (FBI) recruited 900 new agents for counter-terrorism work.

# The United Nations and terrorism

The United Nations (UN) is an organization of countries that was established in 1945 for the purpose of promoting international peace, security and co-operation. Since global terrorism first emerged in the 1960s, the UN has played an important part in getting different countries to agree on how to fight it.

◀ *United Nations weapons inspectors in Iraq in 1998 destroy chemical weapons containing the deadly nerve gas, sarin.*

The UN has staged many debates on terrorism, and has passed more than twenty anti-terrorism treaties and resolutions. These include measures to prevent hijackings, hostage-taking and assassinations. They also include agreements to undermine terrorist activity by restricting the movement of terrorist assets (such as money), and banning the financing or arming of terrorists. The UN also often acts as a voice for international anger following terrorist outrages. It condemns such acts, and calls for sanctions against states that support terrorism.

Not all countries agree with such measures, and so the UN has also been the scene of arguments between nations, especially over the definition of terrorism. Many Islamic countries, for example, would like the definition widened to include the actions taken by Israel against Palestinians in the occupied territories.

The UN does not have the political or military power to enforce these resolutions. It relies on the willingness of individual governments to do so. However, it does play a significant role in encouraging action against terrorism.

FACT:
As well as passing treaties and resolutions, the UN also has organizations and agencies to advise on counter-terrorism methods. For example, the International Civil Aviation Organization suggests how best to meet the threat of hijacks; the International Atomic Energy Agency looks at the security of nuclear material in nuclear power plants; and the World Health Organization advises on what to do in the event of a biological weapons attack.

◀ *A chemical weapons expert checks toxicity levels during a training exercise. In 2002, the World Health Organization published detailed guidelines on how governments should respond to a biological or chemical weapons attack.*

## 6.What is the war on terrorism?

# What happened on 11 September 2001?

Tuesday 11 September 2001 saw the most devastating terrorist attack in history. Two hijacked aircraft crashed into the north and south towers of the World Trade Center in New York City, causing both towers to collapse. A third plane crashed into the Pentagon (the US Department of Defense) in Washington D.C., and a fourth hijacked plane crash-landed in Pennsylvania killing everyone on board. In this carefully planned attack on the symbols of American military and economic power, more than 3,000 people died.

**weblinks**

For more information about the hunt for Osama bin Laden go to www.waylinks.co.uk/series/why/terrorists

▼ *This photo, taken at 9.03 a.m., shows Flight 175, with 65 passengers and crew on board, about to crash into the south tower of the World Trade Center.*

The terrorist organization responsible was Al Qaeda. This is a powerful and very secretive network of Islamic fundamentalist cells co-ordinated by Osama bin Laden. 11 September appeared to be the awful fulfilment of bin Laden's 1998 fatwah (ruling) calling on Muslims to kill Americans. People in the United States were shocked that such an attack could happen in the richest, most well-armed and best-defended country on earth. Many woke up for the first time to the true threat of modern-day terrorism: it is ruthless and can strike anywhere.

One of the most alarming aspects of the 11 September attack was its simplicity. No weapons of mass destruction or hi-tech gadgetry were used. It simply needed a group of terrorists – some of them with piloting skills – armed with small knives who were prepared to sacrifice their lives for their cause. It has raised doubts about many aspects of US homeland defence, including failures in intelligence and domestic airport security in the US and other countries.

▲ *343 New York firefighters died during the destruction of the World Trade Center.*

case study · case study · case study · case study · case study

Mohammed Atta was one of the pilots who flew an aircraft into the World Trade Center. He was possibly the ringleader of the whole attack. He was born in 1968, the son of a successful lawyer, and grew up in a wealthy neighbourhood in Cairo, Egypt. He moved to Germany to study architecture in 1993. Intelligent and well-educated, he did not fit the description of a typical terrorist. Yet his fellow students in Hamburg recall that Atta grew more and more religious during his time there. He started an Islamic prayer group in 1999, which may have been a recruiting place for Islamic militants. He moved to the USA in 2001, where he studied aviation at a Florida flying school. On the morning of 11 September, he and a colleague travelled to Boston and boarded American Airlines Flight 11. In his diary, Atta prepared himself for the moment of his death: 'You should feel complete tranquillity, because the time between you and your marriage in heaven is very short.'

# The military war

The events of 11 September 2001 may have marked a turning point in history. They have led to great changes in Western foreign policy, and especially Western ways of dealing with terrorism. In the weeks and months following the attacks, America and her allies began a 'War on Terrorism'. Several old enemies from the Cold War era, such as the USA, Russia and China, have found themselves on the same side in this new phase of history, as did some Muslim powers, such as Turkey, Tajikistan and Pakistan.

In October 2001, the US led an attack on Al Qaeda bases in Afghanistan and against the Taliban, the Islamic fundamentalist rulers of Afghanistan who refused to hand over Osama bin Laden. By December, the Taliban had been overthrown. The fight against Al Qaeda continued into 2002.

▼ *Two soldiers from the Afghan rebel force, the Northern Alliance, watch as US B-52 bombers attack Taliban positions in northern Afghanistan in November 2001.*

▲ US and Canadian soldiers during a raid to destroy Al Qaeda positions in Afghanistan.

By June, Al Qaeda forces had split into small groups in different parts of the country, making it difficult to find and defeat them. Bin Laden and his top leaders were not found.

Early in 2002, the USA turned its attention to other places where Al Qaeda cells were believed to exist, such as in Pakistan, Georgia, Yemen, Sudan, Somalia, Iraq and the Philippines. For this next stage in the war on terror, American forces, including CIA intelligence agents, were used to advise, train, and provide intelligence and technical assistance to each country. Troops were also able to carry out carefully targeted raids on suspected terrorist hideaways.

> 'The main problem in the last three months of war has been that while the US has destroyed Al Qaeda's terror network, it has not eradicated its members.'
>
> *General Juraat Khan Panjshiri, Afghanistan's national security chief, speaking in May 2002*

**weblinks**

For more information about the USA's war on terrorism go to www.waylinks.co.uk/ series/why/terrorists

# The secret war

A secret war against terrorism was also begun after 11 September. A few weeks after the attacks, the UN passed Resolution 1373, its most wide-ranging anti-terrorism measure to date. The countries that signed up to it agreed to ban the supply of money or arms to known terrorists. They also agreed to freeze terrorist assets in their banks, and to deny a safe haven to terrorists or those who support them. Border controls to restrict the movement of terrorists were introduced. They also promised to give early warning of possible future terrorist acts to other countries.

The US has led the campaign to root out terrorist cells. It has become evident that these cells exist in many of the major cities of Europe and North America. Between September 2001 and March 2002, about 1,000 suspected terrorists were arrested, and at least $80 million in terrorist assets were frozen by more than 140 countries. Even former terrorist-supporting countries like Libya and Sudan have offered to share information on the Al Qaeda network with the USA.

▲ *Mohammed Atta caught on CCTV at Maine Jetport on 11 September 2001. Later that day, he would lead the hijackers on American Airlines Flight 11.*

*A raid by US customs officers in November 2001 on a bank in Minneapolis, Minnesota. The bank was suspected of playing a part in Al Qaeda's worldwide money-transfer network.*

Another focus of the secret war is the world banking system. Modern electronic banking allows large sums of money to flow between bank accounts around the world within a matter of minutes. This makes it easy for terrorist leaders to pay their agents in different countries. A combination of poor business practice and corruption has also allowed terrorists to take advantage of this system for money laundering. In November 2001, the International Monetary Fund (IMF) urged its members to set up 'financial intelligence squads' to look out for suspicious dealings.

FACT:
In March 2002, a joint US-Saudi Arabian operation was carried out to freeze the assets of Al-Haramain Islamic Foundation, a charitable organization accused by the US of using funds to support terrorist groups including Al Qaeda and the Somalia-based Al-Itihaad al-Islamiya. US Treasury Secretary Paul O'Neill called the operation 'a sign of the growing strength of the anti-terror coalition'.

# Terrorists of tomorrow

The war against terrorism is not only about confronting terrorist groups, but also the countries which sponsor them. Some Western states, particularly the USA, are worried about the possibility that anti-Western regimes might supply terrorists with weapons of mass destruction.

In 2002, the US government expressed its concern about the possibility that Saddam Hussein's Iraq was developing chemical and biological weapons, in violation of United Nations resolutions. The US argued that Iraq had links with Al Qaeda – although there was no firm evidence for this – and that it was only a matter of time before these dangerous weapons ended up being used against Western targets.

In November 2002, the UN adopted Resolution 1441 demanding that Iraq provide a complete

▼ *Iraqis surrender to coalition troops during the Iraq War of 2003. The American and British governments insisted their quarrel was with Saddam Hussein, not the people of Iraq. Nevertheless, many Arabs were angered by the invasion, which they saw as an act of Western aggression against a much weaker Muslim country.*

*Osama bin Laden, who avoided capture in the US-led attack on Afghanistan. He spoke to the world in several videos released in late 2001 and early 2002. He remains a hero to many radical young Muslims around the world.*

record of its weapons of mass destruction, and unrestricted access to its weapons sites by an inspection team. Iraq failed to comply with these demands, and in March 2003 US and British forces invaded Iraq. Within weeks, Saddam's regime had been toppled. The invasion, and the loss of civilian life that it led to, was broadcast every night on television, and inflamed large sections of Arab opinion.

The war may serve as a warning to other states that they should stop sponsoring terrorism, or face the consequences. On the other hand, it may bring further instability to the region, and the anger it has bred may inspire a new generation of terrorists.

FACT:
Cyber-terrorism is the name given to terrorist attacks on computer systems. These could be used to disrupt essential services such as transport, hospitals and police. Cyber-terrorist weapons include weapons that use microwaves to destroy electronics. Electromagnetic bombs can create shockwaves up to a thousand times stronger than a lightning strike. More common are computer viruses which attack computer systems by planting harmful programs within them.

# GLOSSARY

**Anarchist**
Somebody who doesn't believe in the need for government, and would like governments to be abolished.

**Arson**
The crime of setting fire to a building or other property.

**Assassination**
The deliberate killing of a public figure, such as a political or military leader.

**Biological weapon**
A missile, bomb or other device used to deliver and spread biological agents that cause disease or death to humans, plants and animals.

**Capitalism**
An economic system based on the private ownership of wealth, characterized by a free market and motivated by profit.

**Cell**
A small group of people who work together. They are often part of a larger group, such as a terrorist organization, but operate independently of other cells.

**Chechen**
One of the native Muslim people of Chechnia, a republic in southwestern Russia. Chechen guerrillas are fighting for their independence from Russia.

**Chemical weapon**
A missile, bomb or other device used to deliver and spread chemical agents, such as a nerve gas or a poison, in order to injure or kill humans, plants and animals.

**Christian Democrat Party**
A conservative political party in Italy. It was the dominant power in most of Italy's governments between 1945 and 1981.

**CIA**
Central Intelligence Agency: a US government agency responsible for intelligence and counter-intelligence activities outside the United States.

**Coalition**
A temporary alliance between two or more groups, such as countries or political parties.

**Cold War**
The state of non-violent conflict between the Soviet Union and the United States and their respective allies between 1945 and 1990.

**Communism**
A political system in which all property and wealth is controlled by the State.

**Computer virus**
A computer program, usually hidden within another harmless-looking program, that damages a computer system, for example by destroying data.

**Counter-terrorism**
Military or political activities intended to combat or prevent terrorism.

**Cyber-terrorism**
A form of terrorism in which computer systems are attacked or threatened.

**Democratic**
Describes a system of government – a democracy – which is ruled by the will of the people. Often used to describe a state in which everyone has equal rights.

**Ethnic**
Relating to a group of people who share the same origins and culture.

**Extortion**
The crime of obtaining something such as money using threats and illegal methods of persuasion.

**Extradition**
The handing over by a government of somebody accused of a crime to a different country for trial or punishment there.

**Extremist**
Somebody who holds extreme political or religious beliefs.

**Fatwah**
A formal religious ruling issued by an Islamic leader.

**Foreign policy**
The programme adopted by a government that defines its attitudes and actions towards other countries and their governments.

**Freedom fighter**
Someone who takes part in an armed uprising against a political system, government or occupying power that they oppose.

**Freezing assets**
Preventing the movement of money or property belonging to a person or organization.

**French Revolution**
A period of violent political upheaval in France between 1789 and 1799. During this time the French monarchy was overthrown.

**Fundamentalism**
A religious movement based on a strict interpretation of holy writings.

**Guillotine**
A machine for executing people by cutting off their heads.

**Hijack**
To take control of a public transport vehicle, especially an aircraft, and hold the people on board as hostages.

**Intelligence**
Information about secret plans or activities, especially those of foreign governments or terrorist groups.

**International Monetary Fund**
An agency of the United Nations that seeks to promote international co-operation between countries on financial matters.

**Investment**
The outlay of money with the object of making a profit, or in

the hope of getting a benefit from it.

**Left-wing**
Supporting the idea of political or social changes and reform.

**Militants**
People who actively support a cause, sometimes using violent methods to achieve their aims.

**Money laundering**
Passing illegally obtained money through a legal business or bank account so as to hide its origins.

**Nationalism**
The desire of a people or nation to achieve political independence, especially by a country under foreign control or by a people with a separate identity but not a state of their own in which to live.

**Nuclear weapon**
A missile or bomb with huge explosive power based on nuclear fission – the splitting of an atom's nucleus into smaller fragments.

**Opium**
A drug derived from the brownish extract from the unripe seedpods of a kind of poppy. It contains highly addictive substances such as morphine and codeine. The morphine in opium is used in the manufacture of heroin.

**Oppressive**
Harsh or cruelly dominating.

**Patriotic**
Describes someone who is proud of their country.

**Radioactive**
Emitting energy in the form of streams of particles due to the decaying of unstable atoms. Elements such as uranium and plutonium are radioactive.

**Real IRA**
A splinter group of the IRA (Irish Republican Army) formed in 1998. The Real IRA are opposed to the peace process and the IRA ceasefire in Northern Ireland. They are dedicated to removing British forces from Northern Ireland using violent means.

**Resolution**
The process of finding agreement and making peace between conflicting sides in a dispute.

**Revolutionary**
Causing or supporting the overthrow of a government or political system.

**Right-wing**
Supporting the idea of keeping social and political systems as they are.

**Sanctions**
Measures taken by one or more nations to apply pressure on another nation to conform to international opinion, for example by ceasing to trade with it.

**Sarin**
An extremely poisonous gas that attacks a person's central nervous system, causing convulsions and eventually death.

**Satellite photography**
Pictures taken by spy satellites that orbit the earth.

**Soviet Union**
A federation of communist states, including Russia, that existed in eastern Europe and north and central Asia from 1917 to 1991.

**State-sponsored terrorism**
Terrorism that is supported by governments. Sponsorship can include the provision of funds, weapons, equipment, training or sanctuary.

**Strategy**
A carefully worked-out plan of action to achieve a goal, such as victory in a war.

**Surveillance**
Continued observation of a person or group who are suspected of illegal actions.

**Treaty**
A formal contract or agreement that is negotiated between countries and signed by all the parties involved.

**Weapons of mass destruction**
Chemical, biological and nuclear weapons.

**World Health Organization**
An agency of the United Nations that helps countries improve their health services and co-ordinates international action against diseases and other threats to health.

## FURTHER INFORMATION

### BOOKS TO READ
*21st Century Debates: Terrorism* by Alex Woolf (Hodder Wayland, 2003)
*Ideas of the Modern World: Communism* by Nigel Richie (Hodder Wayland, 2000)
*Key Concepts: Terrorism* by John Gearson (Polity Press, 2003)
*Lives in Crisis: Conflict in Northern Ireland* by R. G. Grant (Hodder Wayland, 2001)
*Points of View: Terrorism* by Alison Jamieson (Wayland, 1991)
*Troubled World: The Arab-Israeli Conflict* by Ivan Minnis (Heinemann Library, 2001)
*Troubled World: The Troubles in Northern Ireland* by Ivan Minnis (Heinemann Library, 2002)
*What's At Issue: War and Conflict* by Sean Connolly (Heinemann Library, 2002)

### WEBSITES
For websites that are relevant to this book, go to www.waylinks.co.uk/series/why/terrorists

# INDEX